This book belongs to:

_____

Written By Yvonne Griffith Orr
Illustrated By Jean Griffith Barrow

Text Copyright © 2023 by Yvonne Griffith Orr
Illustrations and Cover Art Copyright © 2023 by Jean Griffith Barrow
An Orr Publishing Book

Summary:
Praying With Papa captures a father's love and devotion for his child. The child becomes aware after saying their nightly prayer. She looks at the
neon picture of the boy and his dog kneeling in prayer. The picture glows in the dark from the dim light of the lamp. She looks at the words. What is
soul? Who is Lord? She begins to question the picture hanging on the wall. Wondering what the prayer is saying, she decides to get clarity from Papa.
Share this sacred teachable moment as Papa answers her questions.

Subjects: CYAC: 1. Juvenile Non-Fiction 2. Memoir 3. African-American values 4. Belizean Creole Culture/ Tradition 5. Religious 6. Father-Child
Relationship CYAC 7. Picture book for Boys and Girls.

Library of Congress Control Number: 2023901492
LCCN Imprint: Orr Publishing, New York
10 9 8 7 6 5 4 3 2 1

Printed in the United States Of America
First Edition: June 2023
Identifier:
Paperback ISBN # 979-8-9866131-1-6
eBook ISBN # 979-8-9866131-1-6
Hardcover ISBN # 979-8-9866131-2-3

Disclaimer:
This book is the author's memories and experiences growing up in Belize.
Any references to Historical events, real people, and places are taken from Wikipedia-Belizean Creole.
The Prayer, " Now I lay me down to sleep." is an old 1700 New England Primer Prayer.
RE: Wikipedia
Book Design By Jamaal Orr
Art Style: Realism
Ages 3-9

ORR PUBLISHING

Dedication

I am giving The LORD Praise and Glory for answered prayers.
He allowed me to achieve this goal.

This book is dedicated to my father, John Foster, who was loving and compassionate. He taught me to love myself, love others, and above all, love The Lord.

I still remember him saying, "Yvonne did you say your prayer?"
Next, to my sons Brian and Jamaal, who encouraged me to share this experience with others. They also grew up with this prayer in their bedrooms. I thank you both for listening, editing, and computer assistance.

I am forever grateful to Carline Constant, my friend, who not only inspired me to publish this book; she guided me through the process. Your calls and media instructions were valuable. This experience taught me it is never too late to learn new things.

Finally, to all fathers, mothers, parents, and grandparents who spend time with their children praying, reading, eating, and playing. Yes, playing, there is an inner child in all of us. We say children are our future; therefore, we are all obligated to nurture and protect them.

"Children are a gift from The Lord; they are a reward from Him."
Psalm 127: 3

PRAYING WITH PAPA:

A Father's Love

Written by Yvonne Griffith Orr

Illustrated by Jean Griffith Barrow

ORR PUBLISHING

My first memory was at
the age of three, praying

every night with my
Papa. I knelt in front of
my bed,

which was pushed
against the wall.

On the wall hung a
neon picture of a boy,
and his

dog kneeling in prayer,
that said;

"Now I lay me
down to sleep,

I pray the Lord
my soul to keep.

If I should die
before I wake,

I pray the Lord
my soul to take."

Every night I rattled off this prayer.

"Now I lay me down to sleep,

I pray the Lord my soul to keep.

If I should die before I wake.

I pray the Lord my soul to take."

Feeling very proud, after saying my prayer,
I gave my Mama a hug and a kiss.

Papa tucked me in bed, gave me a kiss, and said;
"Good night, my Precious Angel."
"Good night Papa, good night Mama," I said.
Papa lowered the kerosene lamp.

The picture on the wall of the boy and his dog kneeling in prayer with the printed words glowed in the dark; because of the reflection of the soft dim light from the lamp.

Every night after the nightly ritual of prayer, I wondered.

Who is the Lord to keep my soul?

Soul! What is a soul?

Where is my soul?

What is it to die?

I'll have to ask Papa.

One night before prayer,
I asked.

"Papa, who is The Lord?"
He quickly responded,

"My sweet baby girl,
The Lord is God, He is
everyone's Father."

"Is He Our Father who
lives in Heaven?"

This question repeated
from The Lord's Prayer.

A prayer frequently said by
my parents.

"Papa! What is a soul?"

"Your soul lives inside you, near your heart.

God lives there too."

I immediately touched my chest, feeling my heart pounding.

"Papa, will He keep your soul, too?"

I was making sure my Papa was always with me.

"Of course, The Lord will keep my soul," he answered.

"Mama's soul too?"

"Yes Mama's too."

"Papa, what is it to die?"

"Die is when you stop breathing, and your soul goes to heaven."

"Papa, I love God."

"God loves you too."

I jumped out of bed and gave Mama
a hug and a kiss.
"Good night, Mama; I love you."
"Good night, Princess; I love you too," Mama said.

"Papa, it's time to say my prayer."

I knelt in front of my bed and said,

"Now I lay me down to sleep.

I pray The Lord my soul to keep.

If I should die before I wake;

I pray The Lord my soul to take."

Feeling excited, I gave Papa a tight hug.

Papa tucked me in
bed and said,

"Good night, my
Precious Angel; I
love you. I want
you to promise me
something."

"PROMISE you what,
Papa?"

"Always remember,
God loves you more."

"Yes, Papa, I promise!

Good night Papa; I love you too," I said.

That was my first of many Religious lessons.

My questions answered to my satisfaction,

the soothing quiet of sleep stole this innocent soul until morning light.

About the Author

❧ ❦ ❧

Ms. Yvonne Griffith Orr was born in Punta Gorda Town, Belize.

She attended St. Peter Claver Elementary and High School.

Before migrating to the United States, she was blessed to teach at the same school she attended.

She is the mother of two sons, Brian and Jamaal, and grandmother of Brian Jr.

Ms. Orr earned a Bachelor of Arts in Elementary Education at Brooklyn College and a Master Of Arts at Adelphi University.

Teacher Yvonne, as she's affectionately called, has always aspired to be an author of children's books.

Now that she is retired from the NYC Department of Education Public School, she is able to write her first published book.

Praying With Papa is a memoir of her growing up in PG, Belize.

About the Illustrator

Ms. Jean Griffith Barrow was born in Belize City. She attended Belize Technical College, where she earned GCE in Visual Art.

Jean's artistic talent was discovered at age two by her mom, Ms. Marie. Her dad, Allan, nurtured this talent by supplying her with enough paper, crayons, and paint, allowing her to express herself.

From 1994 - 1996 she sculpted miniature figurines depicting the lifestyle of Belizeans in the early 1900 and beyond.

"Old Belize " was a successful show presented at the Bliss Institute in Belize City.

Today, Ms.Jean lives with her daughter Jenene in The United States and continues her art projects.

Let's begin your Memoir; it's your turn:

A Memoir is a memory of an experience, something that happened to you.

1. What do you remember?

Draw a picture below of a memory of yours spending time with a family member.

2. List the details you remember about this memory?

_____

_____

_____

_____

_____

_____

_____

The Creole People of Belize

The author and illustrator of this book, "Praying With Papa," were born in British Honduras, present-day Belize.

Ms. Yvonne and Ms. Jean decided to collaborate to share their rich Belizean Creole Culture. Although they grew up in Belize during the sixties, most Belizean families try to maintain their ethnicity. Belize is the home of many ethnic groups, which include Creole, Maya, Garifuna, East Indian, and Mestizo.

The Creole or Kriol people of Belize are of West African ancestry by way of Jamaica and Miskito Coast. The British and Scottish logwood cutters who settled along the Bay of Honduras called themselves Baymen.

[1] Many settlers from the Miskito Coast brought enslaved people with them to the new settlement, Belize Town. The primary purpose was to cut and export logwood from the dense rainforest.

In Belize Town, the Creole people created a lingua, a mixture of African, English, and Miskito languages.[2] They started their own villages along the Belize River.

Today, the Creole language is predominantly spoken throughout Belize. This ethnic group which comes from the Igbo Tribe, has their own beliefs and lifestyle.

Later, influenced by colonialism, many became Christians. The first churches in Belize were Presbyterian, Roman Catholic, and Methodist.[3] Children attended Christian schools; Bible reading and praying were part of the curriculum. Belize is still known as a Christian Nation.

* 1 2 3 Wikipedia

Thank you for your purchase!

If you enjoyed reading this story, please leave a review. We read every review, and they help new readers discover our books.

Also, look out for the Praying With Papa Coloring and Activity Workbook!